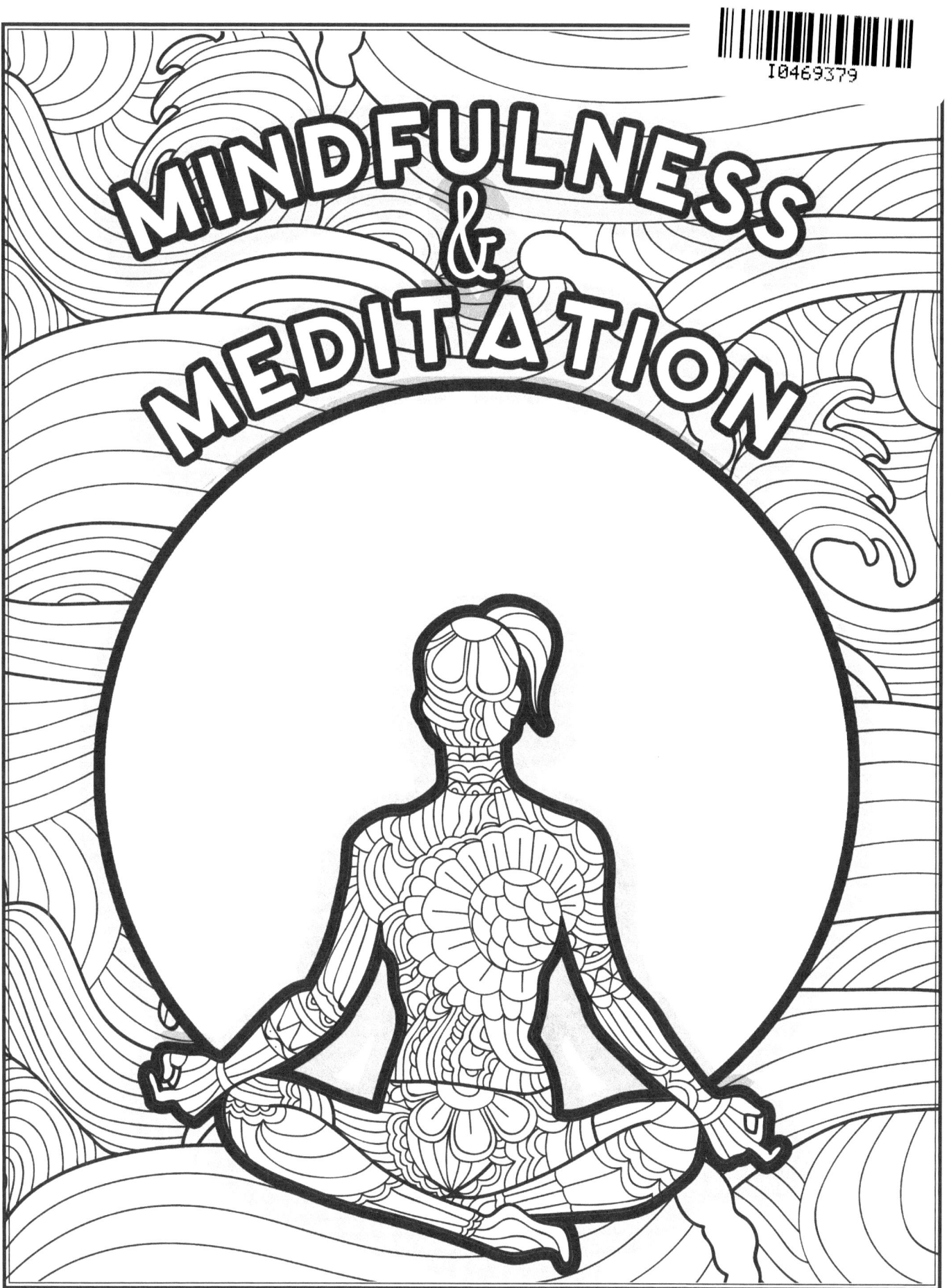

MINDFULNESS & MEDITATION

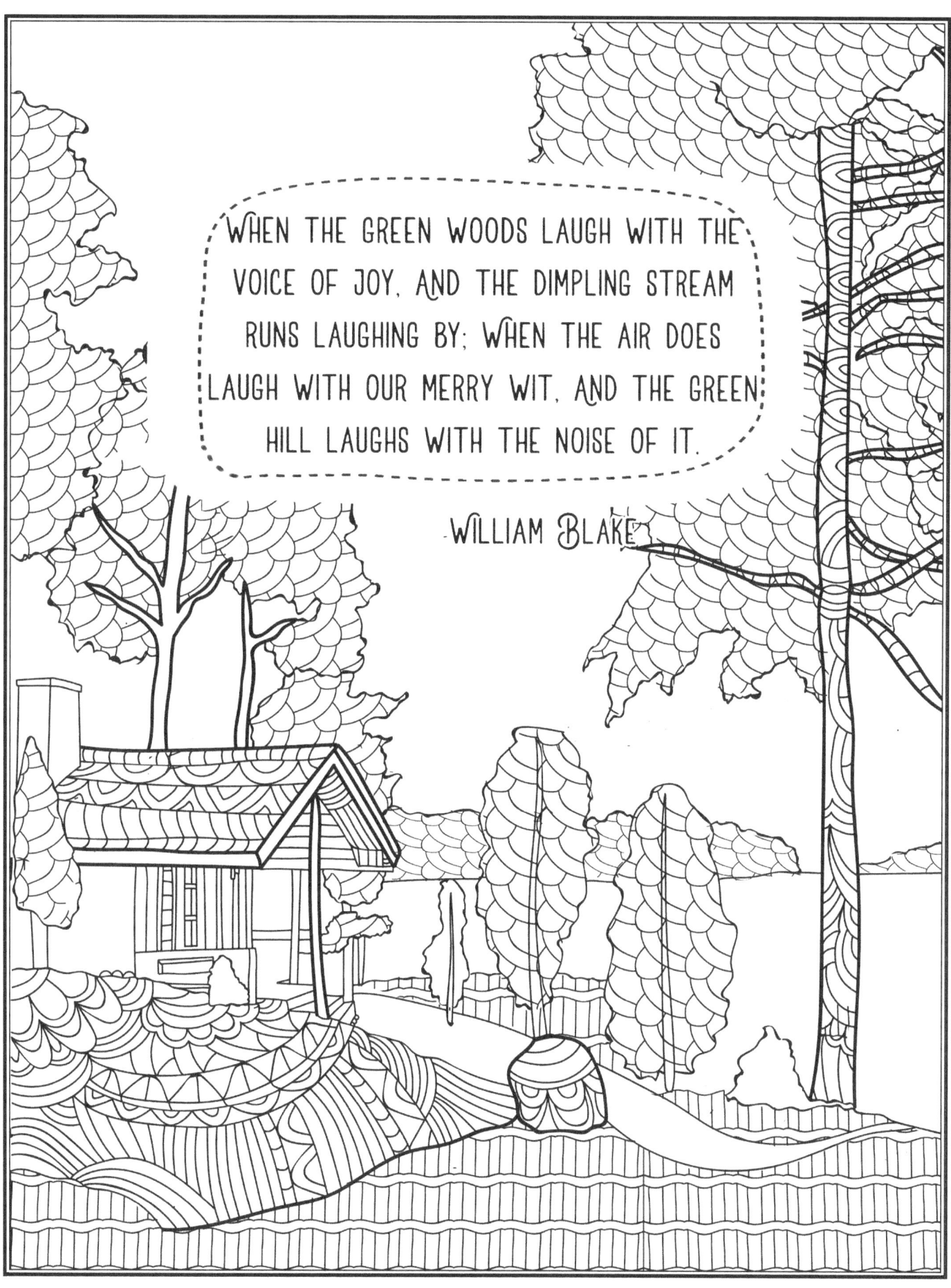

I long for the countryside. That's where I get my calm and tranquillity - from being able to come and find a spot of green.

- Emilia Clarke

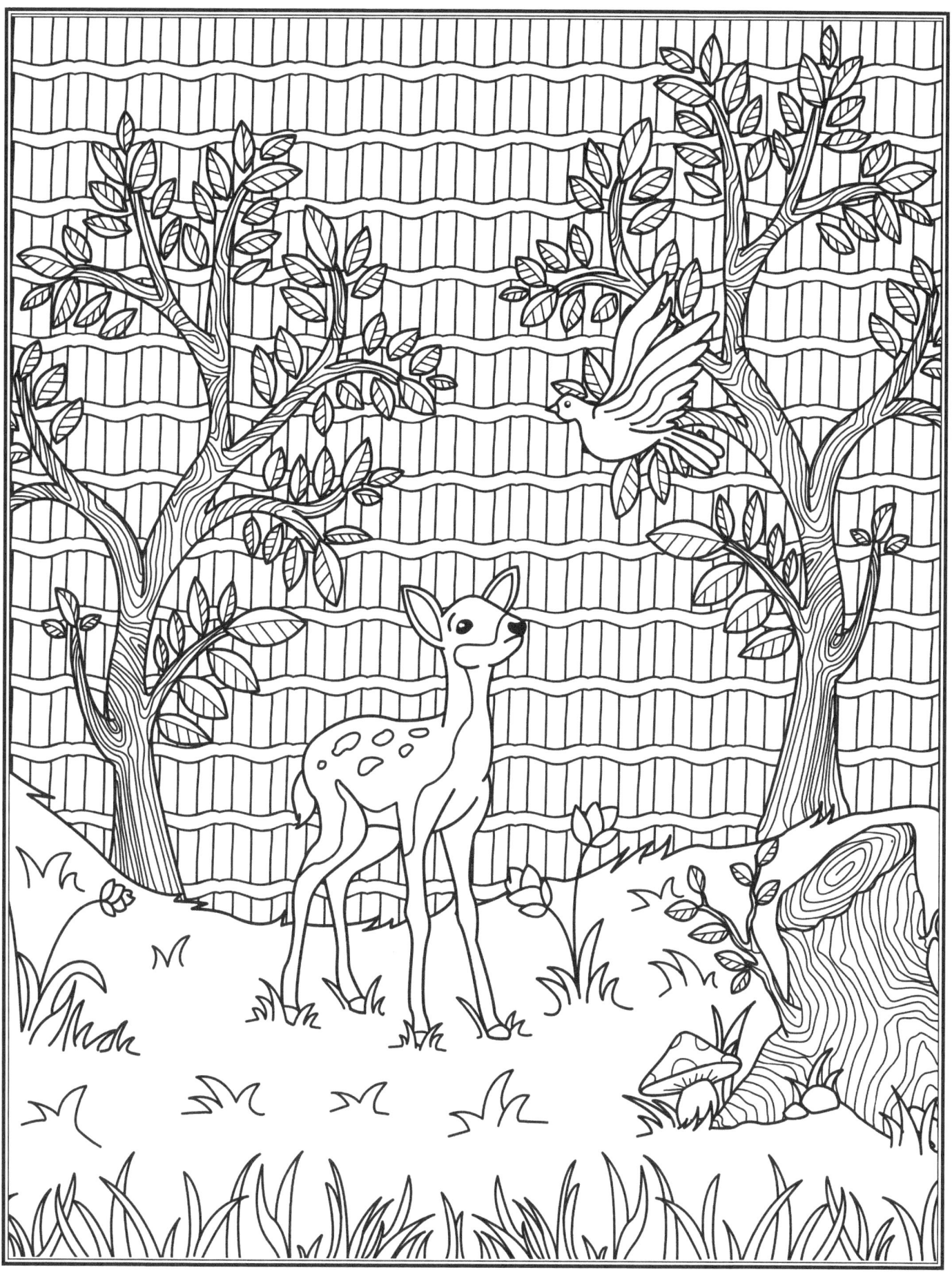

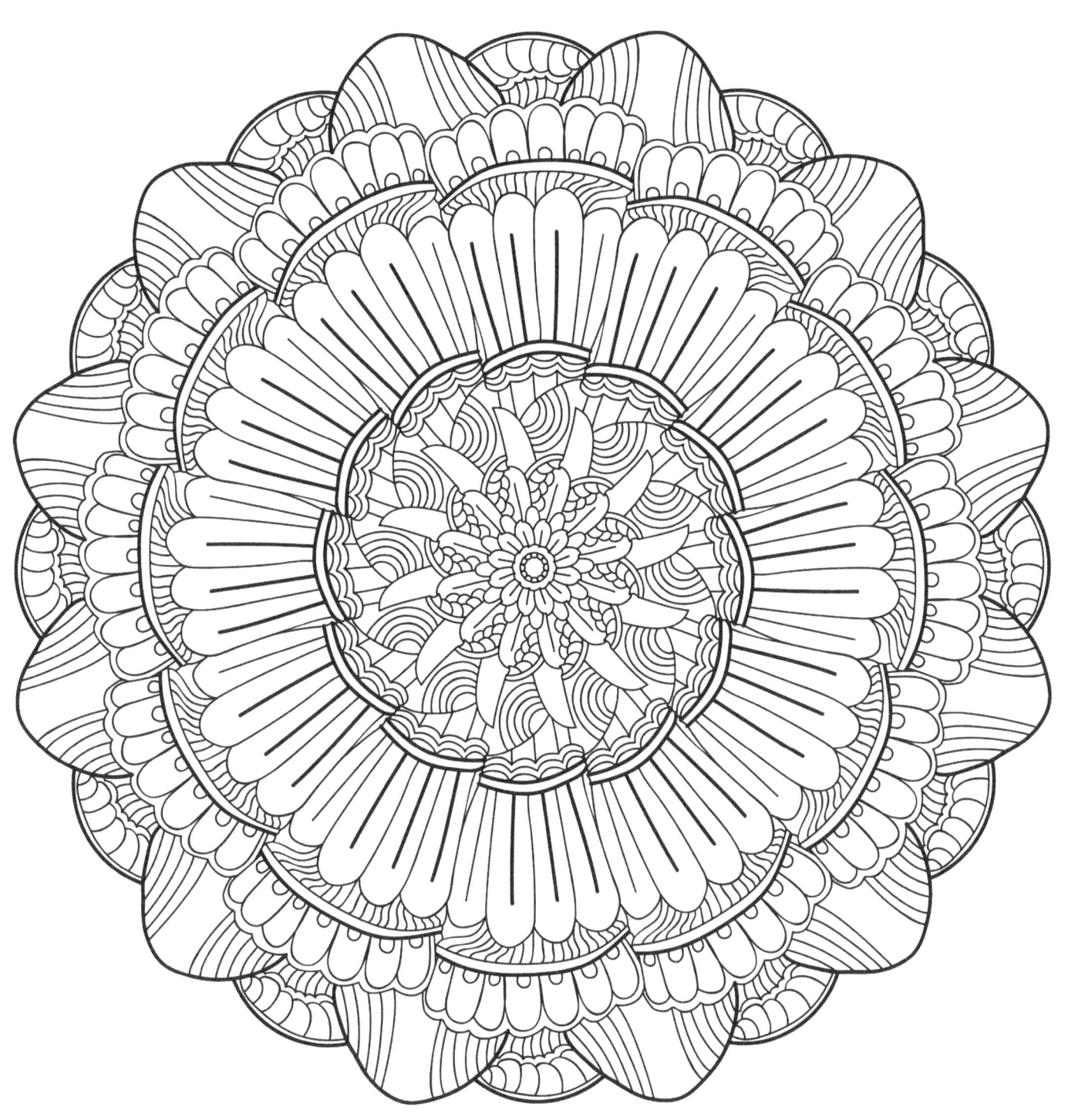

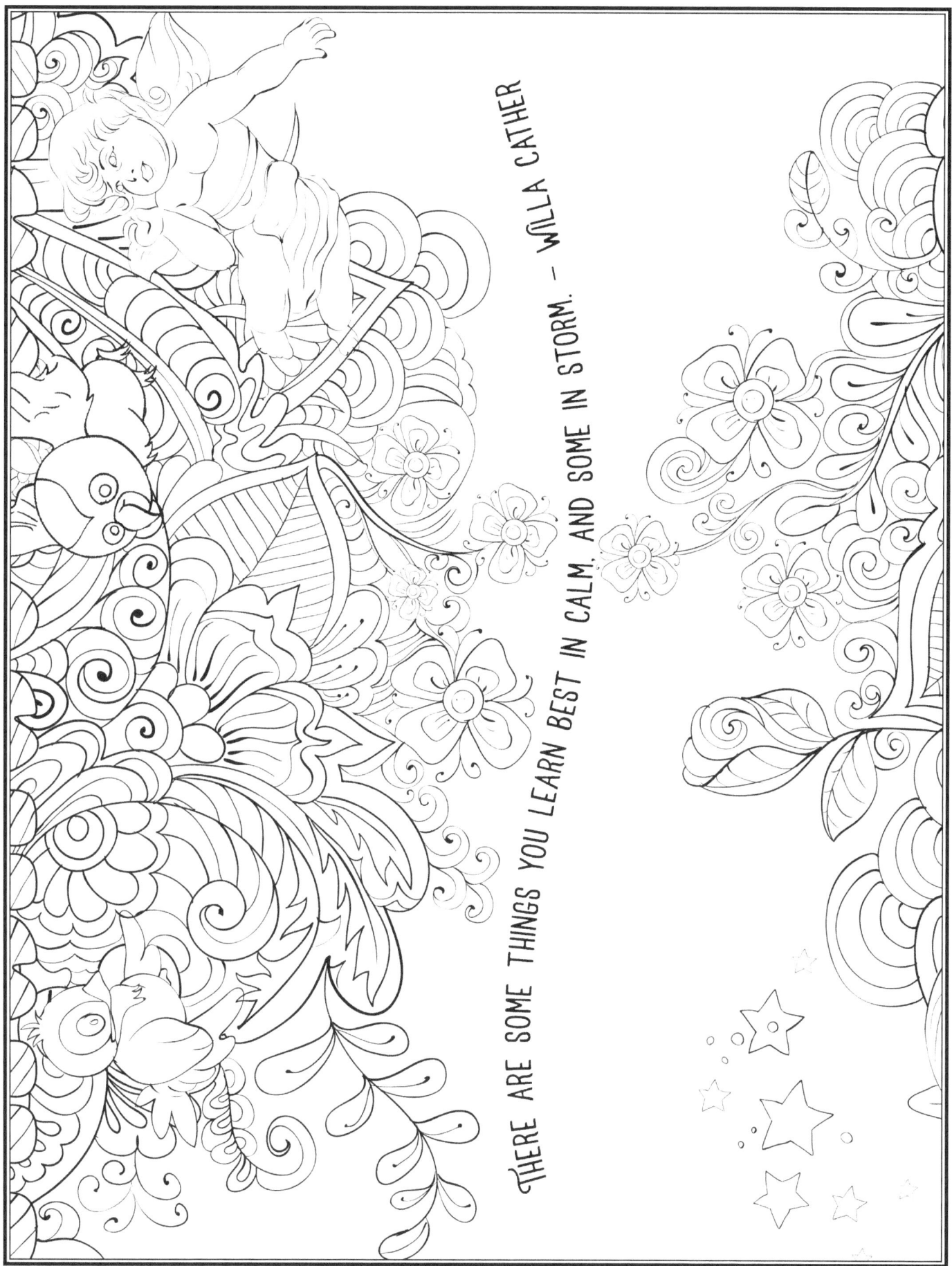

THERE ARE SOME THINGS YOU LEARN BEST IN CALM, AND SOME IN STORM. — WILLA CATHER

Green is the prime color of the world, and that from which its loveliness arises.

- Pedro Calderon de la Barca

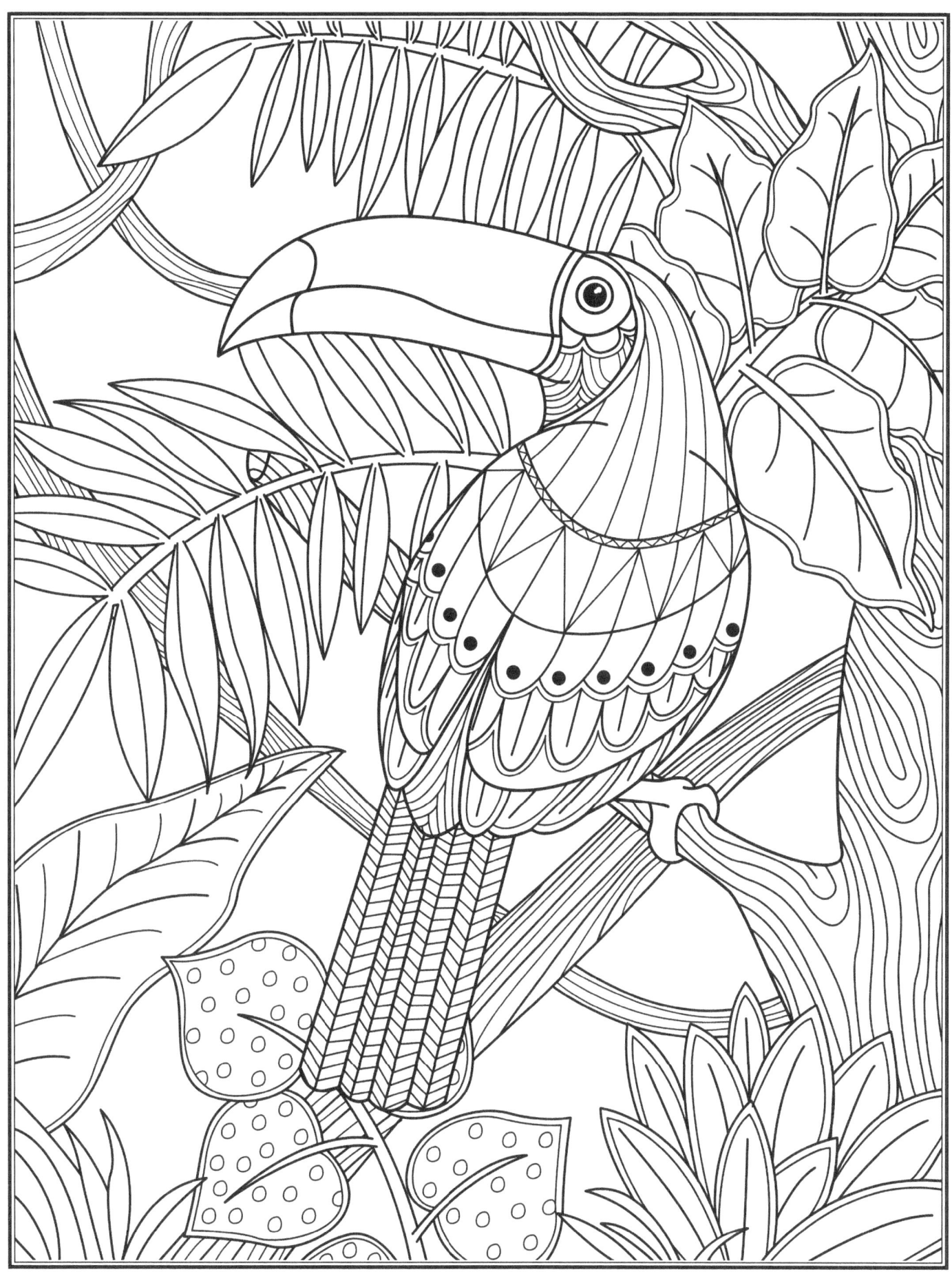

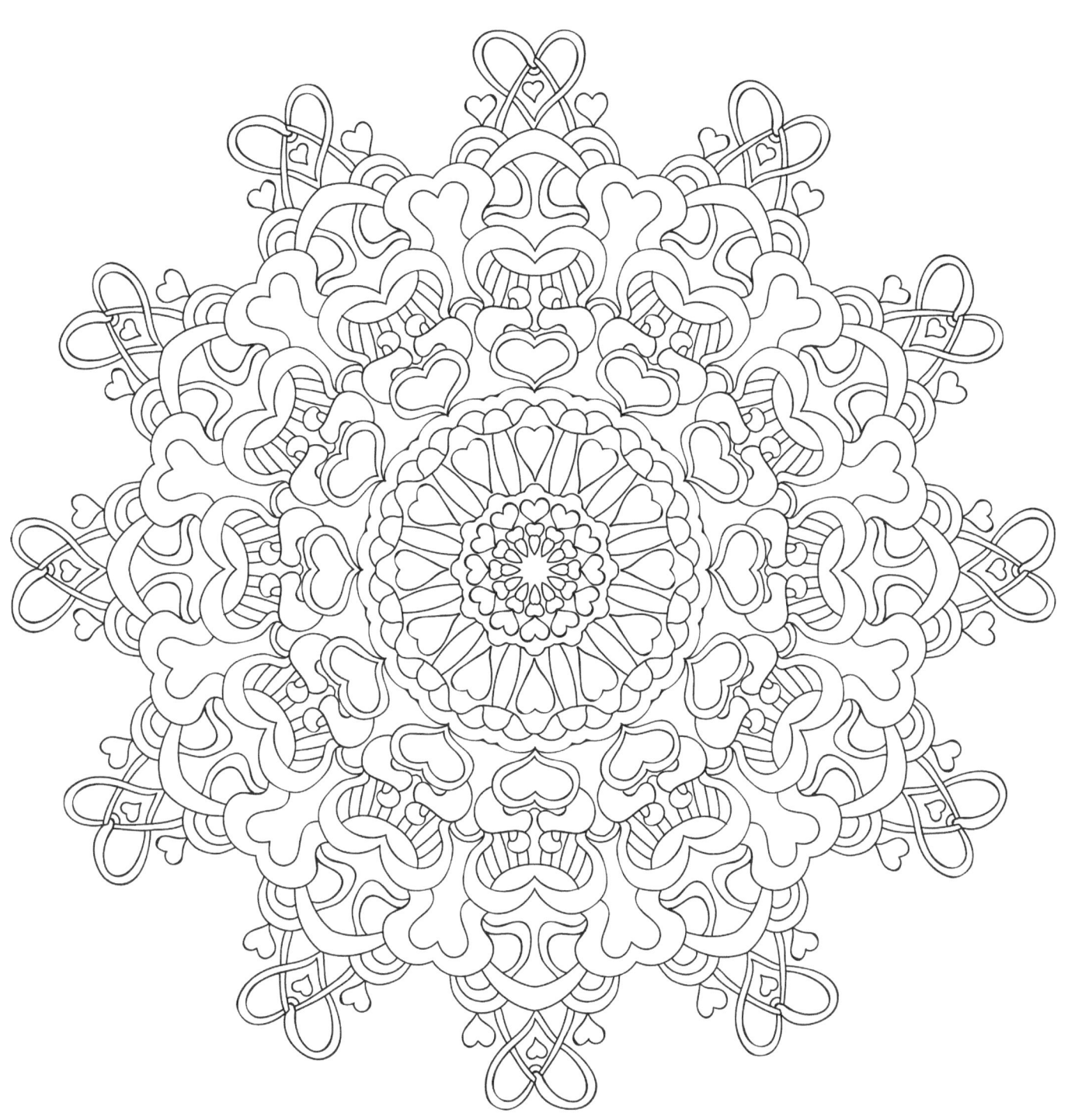

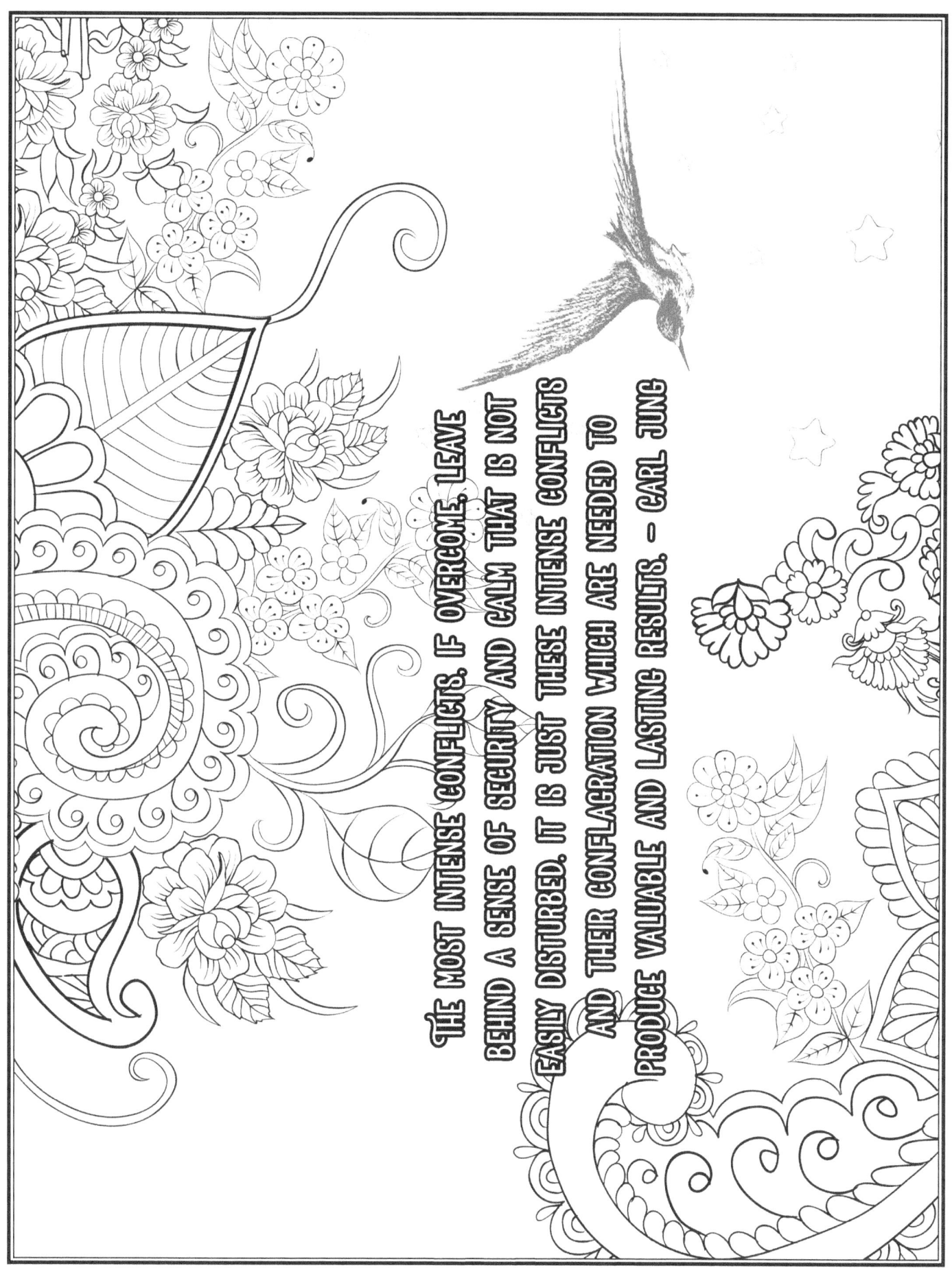

THE MOST INTENSE CONFLICTS, IF OVERCOME, LEAVE BEHIND A SENSE OF SECURITY AND CALM THAT IS NOT EASILY DISTURBED. IT IS JUST THESE INTENSE CONFLICTS AND THEIR CONFLAGRATION WHICH ARE NEEDED TO PRODUCE VALUABLE AND LASTING RESULTS. - CARL JUNG

I like to be lazy. I do like to be busy and really active, but when that's done, you can be sure I will be a lazy boy. I like to take time and relax and enjoy life.

-Olivier Theyskens

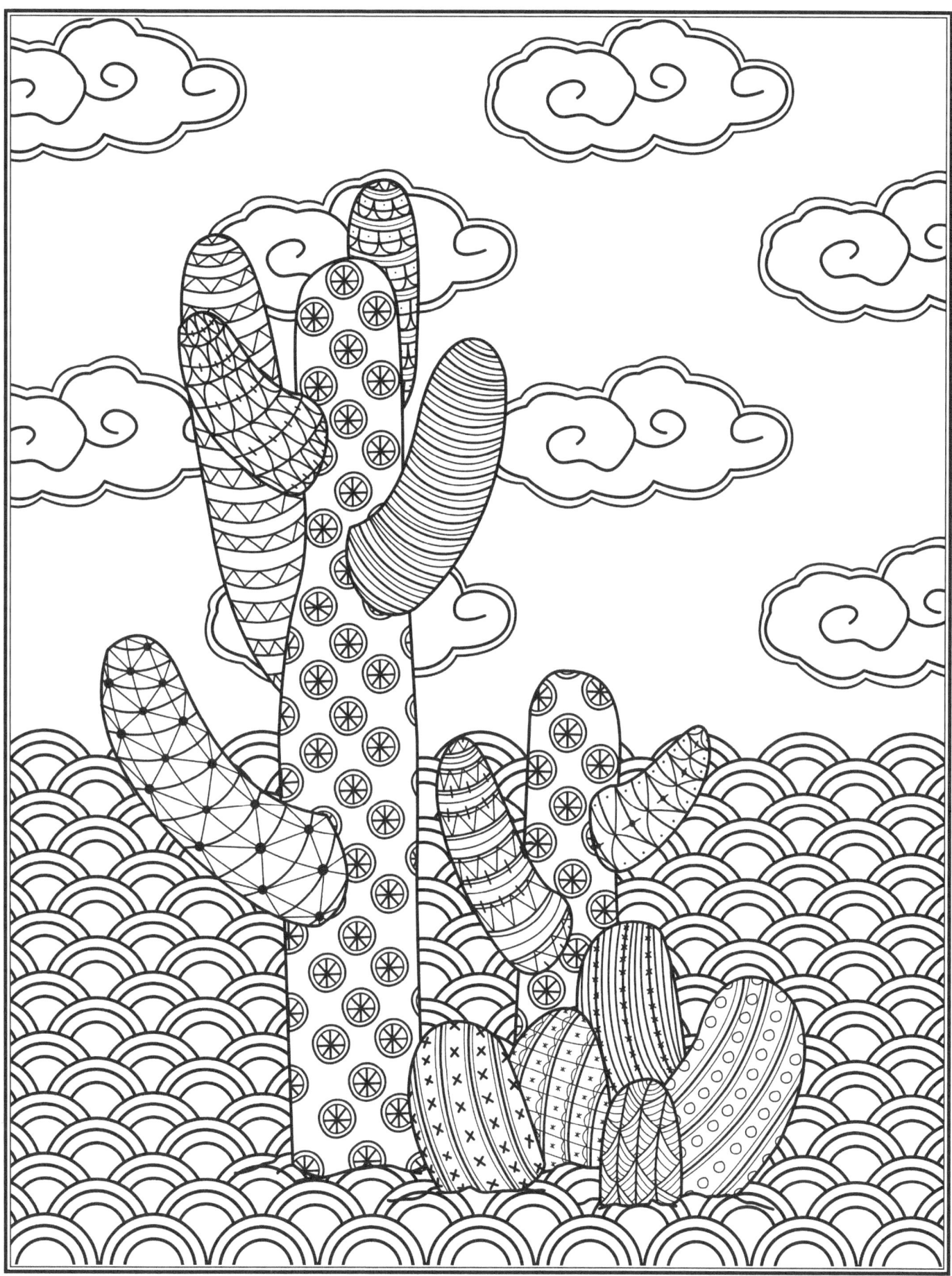

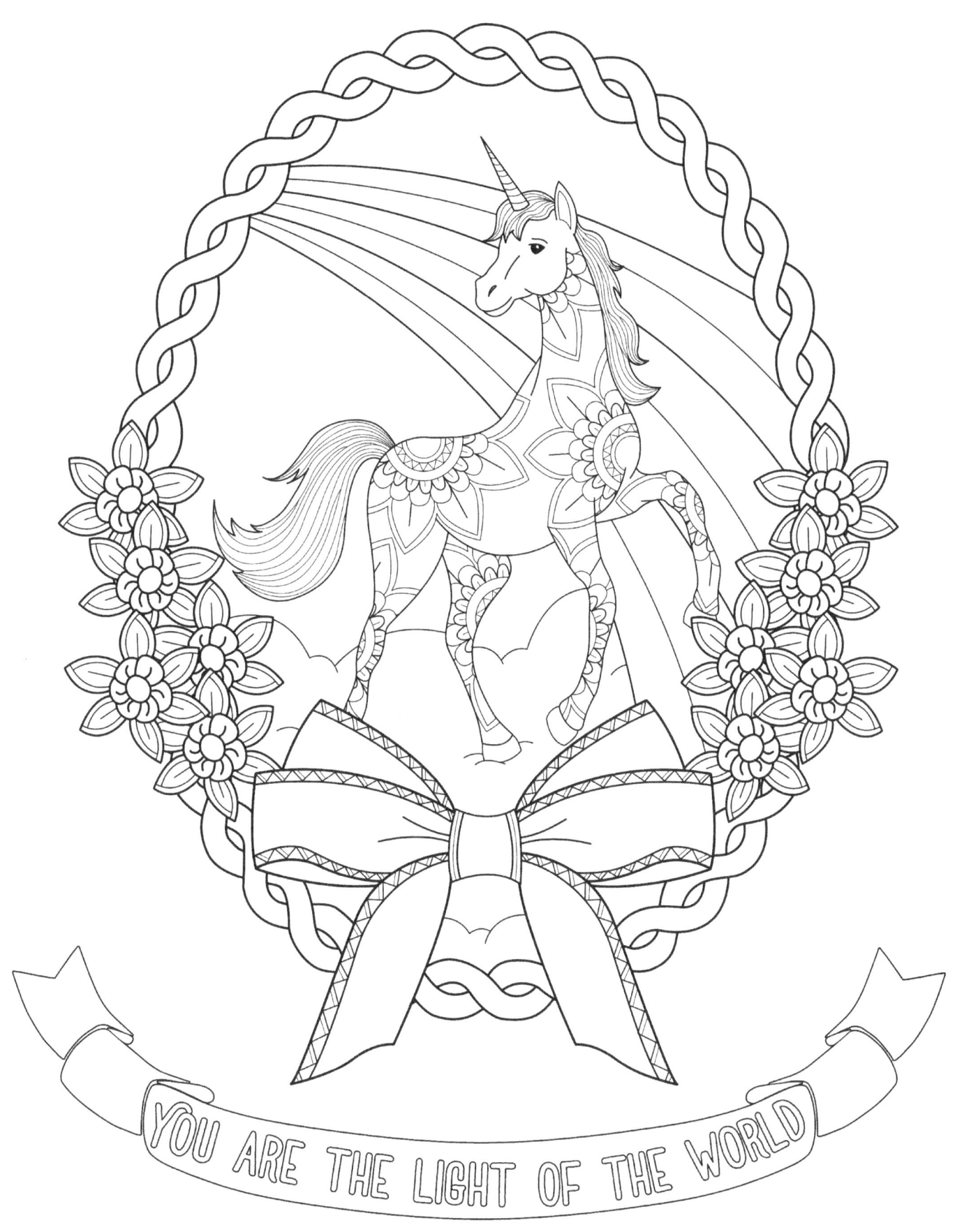

The time to relax is when you don't have time for it.

-Sydney J. Harris

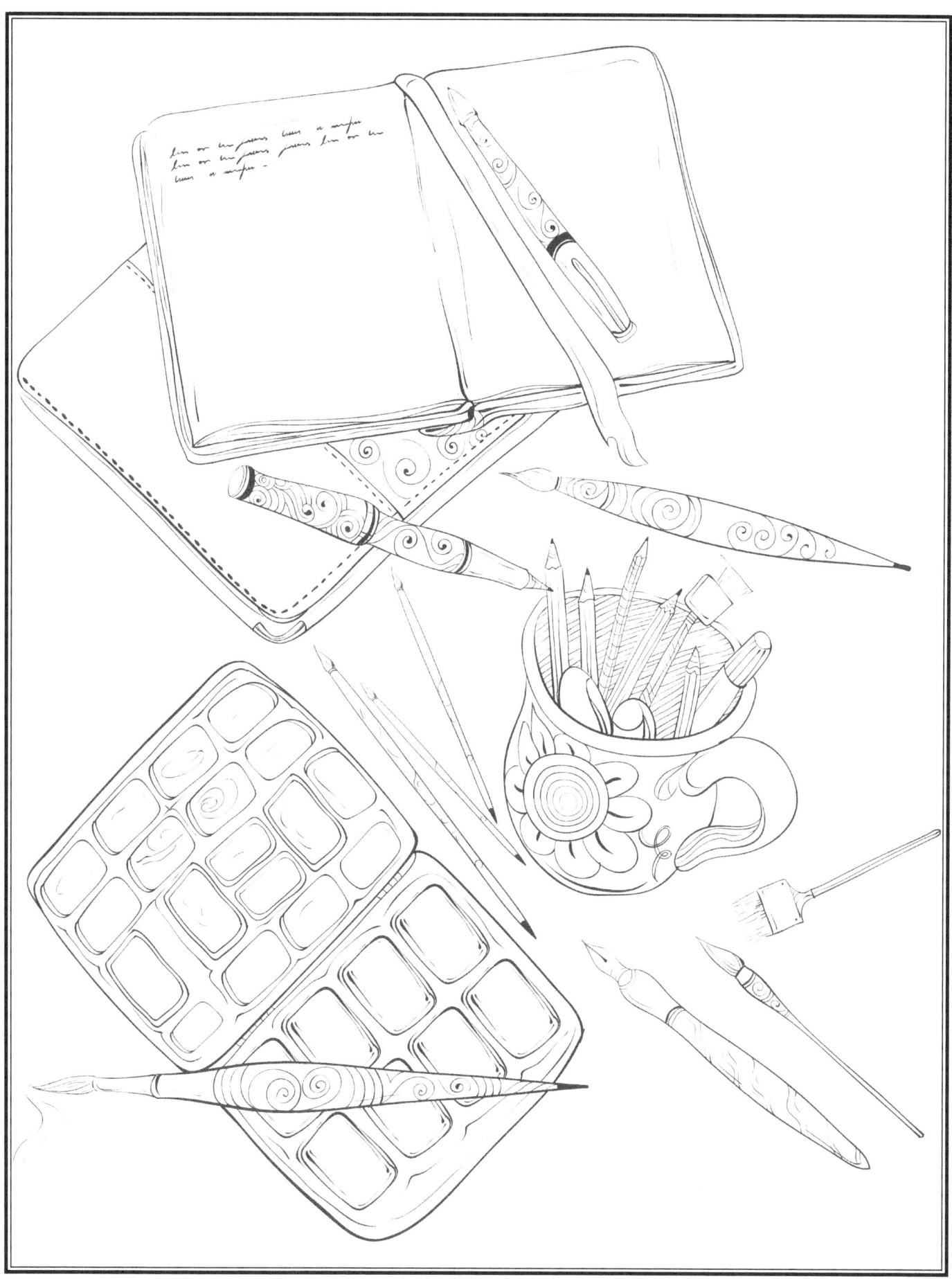

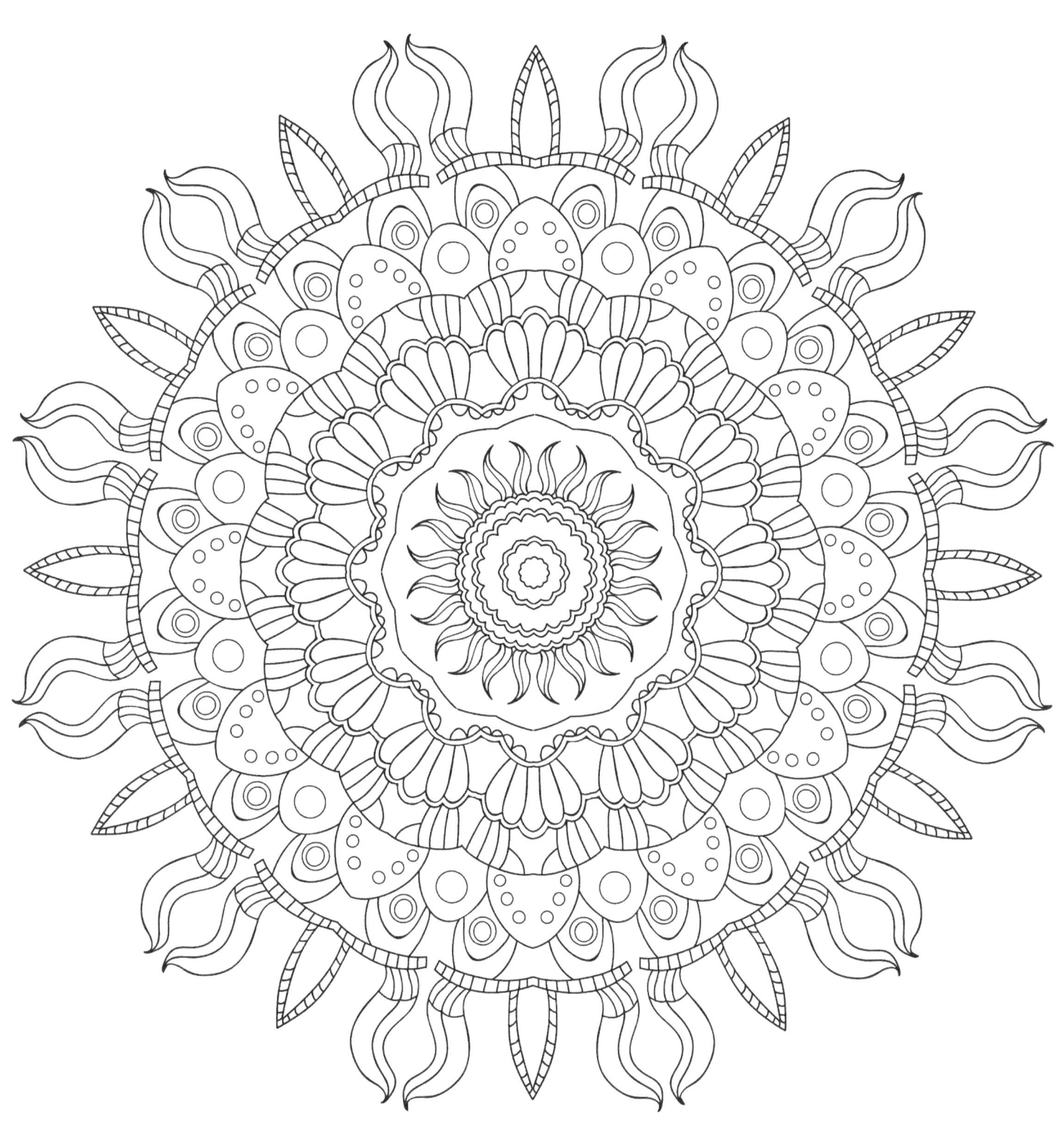

24

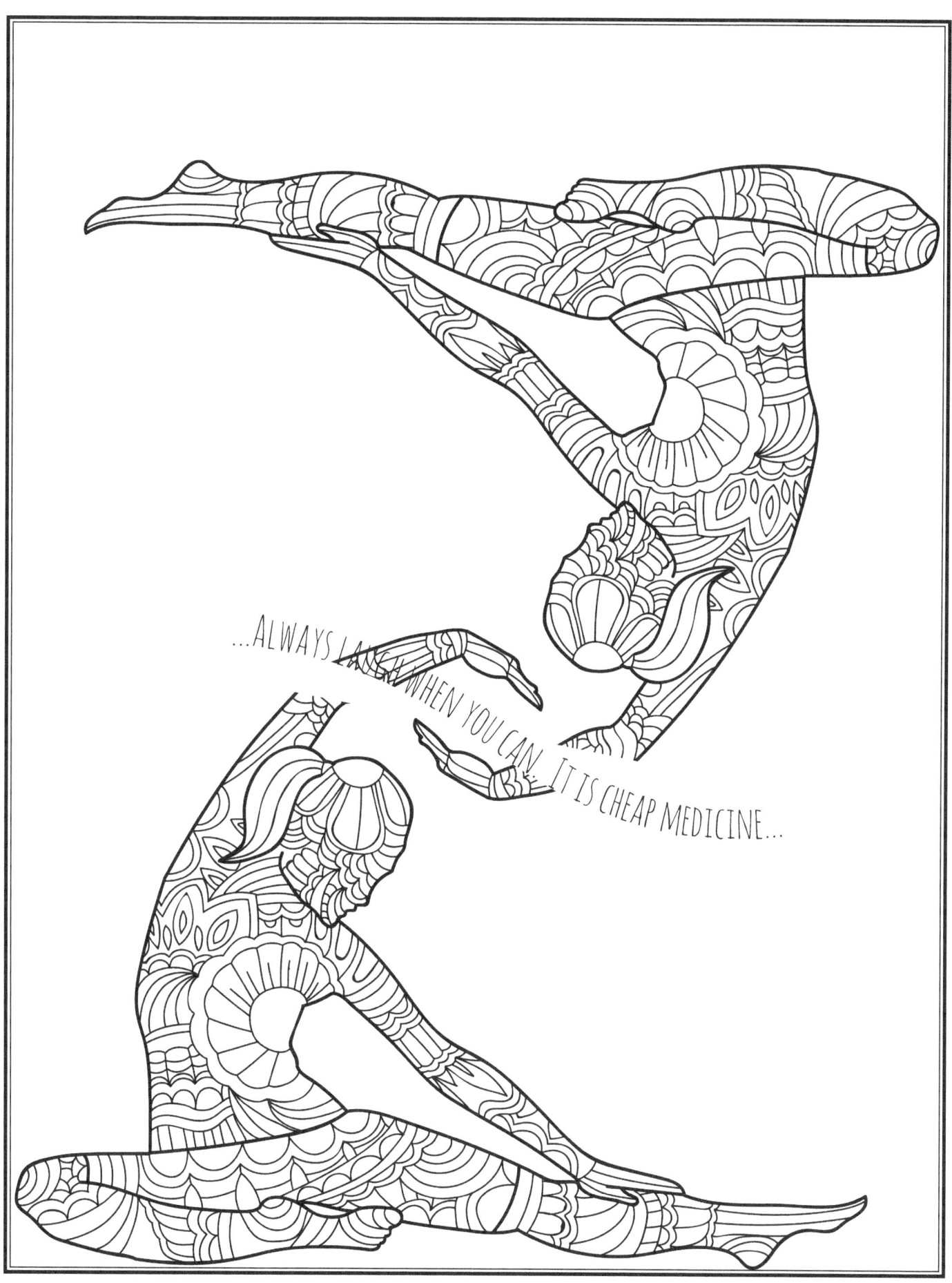

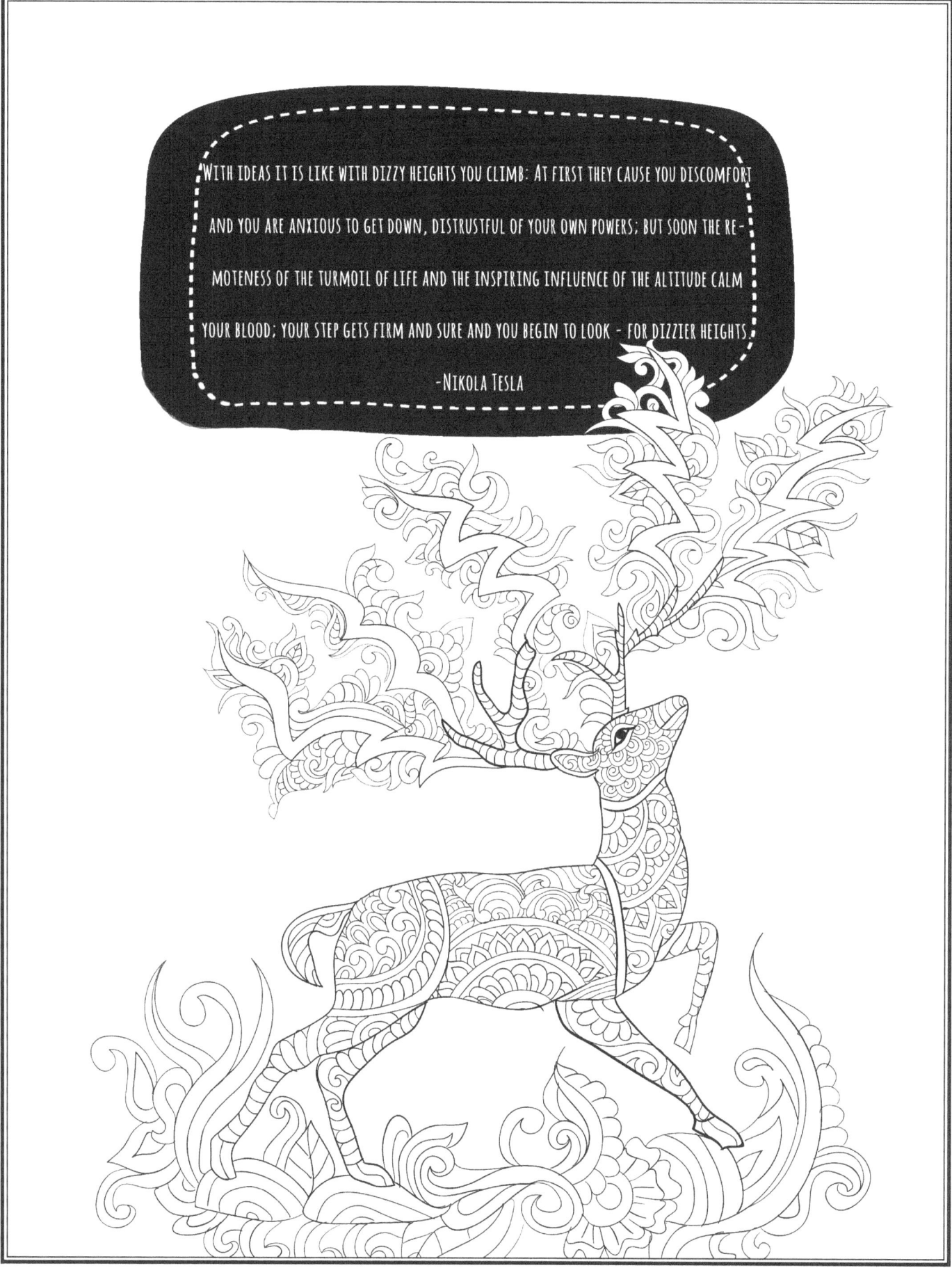

Stop a minute, right where you are. Relax your shoulders, shake your head and spine like a dog shaking off cold water. Tell that imperious voice in your head to be still.

-Barbara Kingsolver

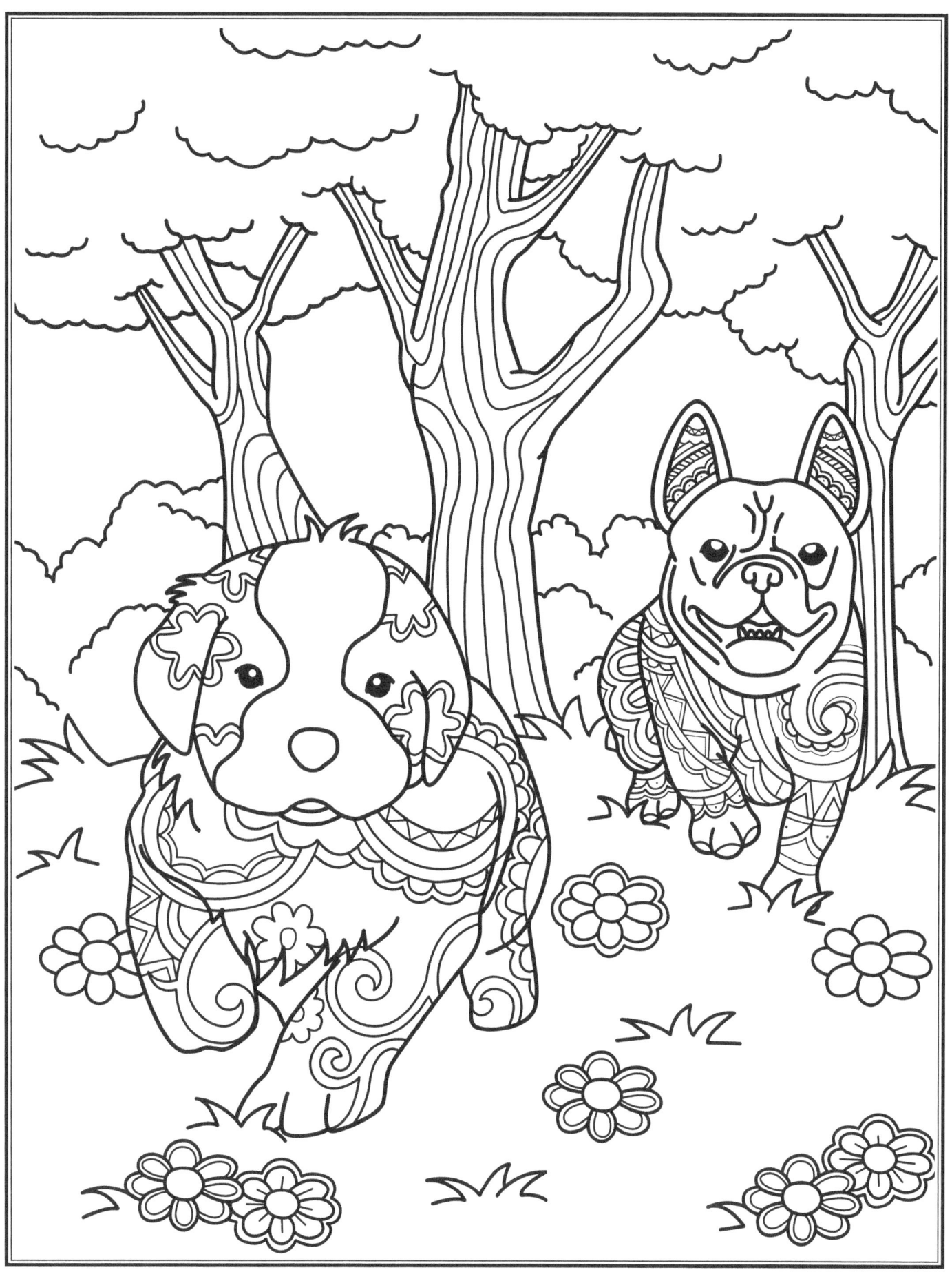

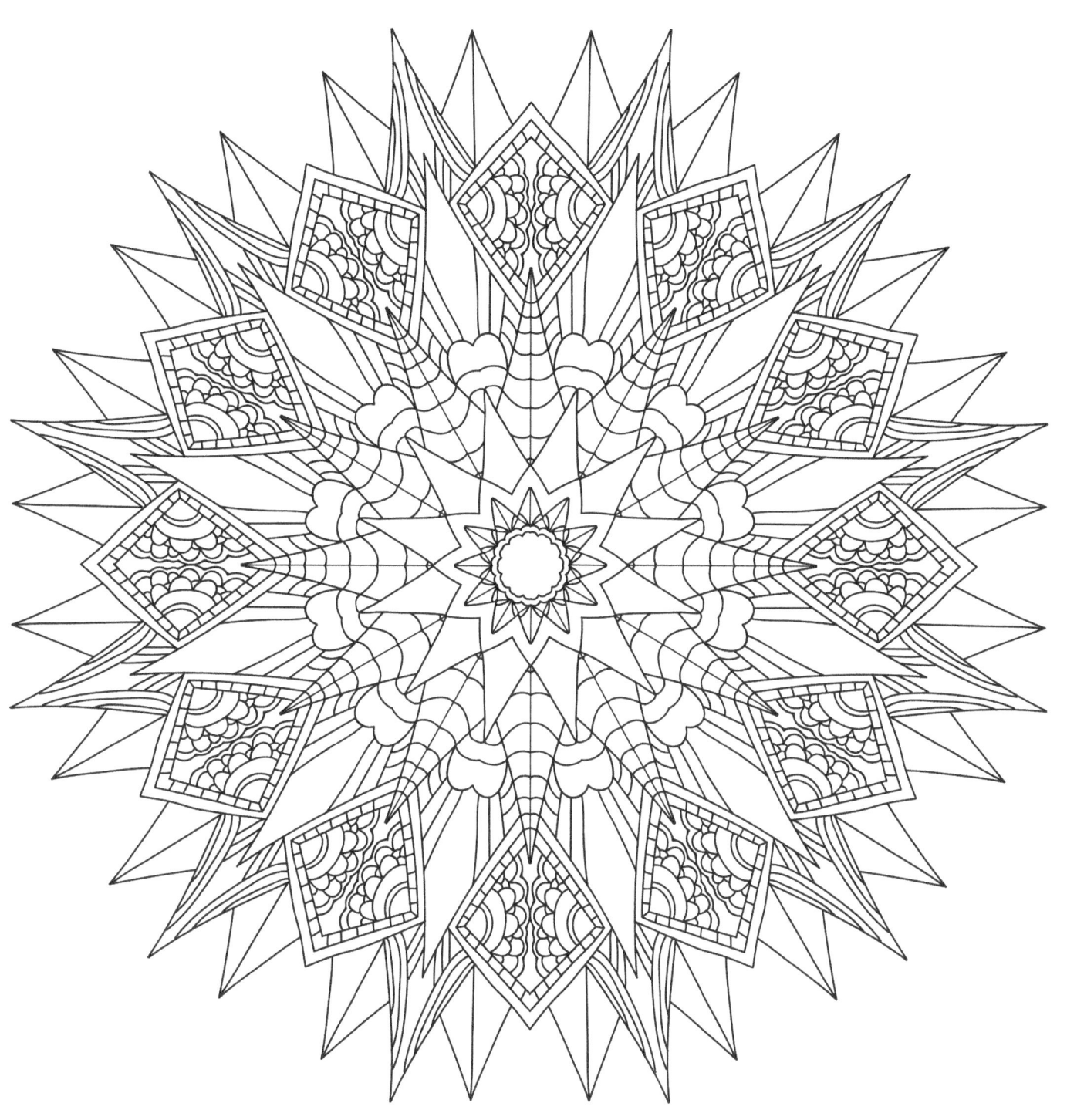

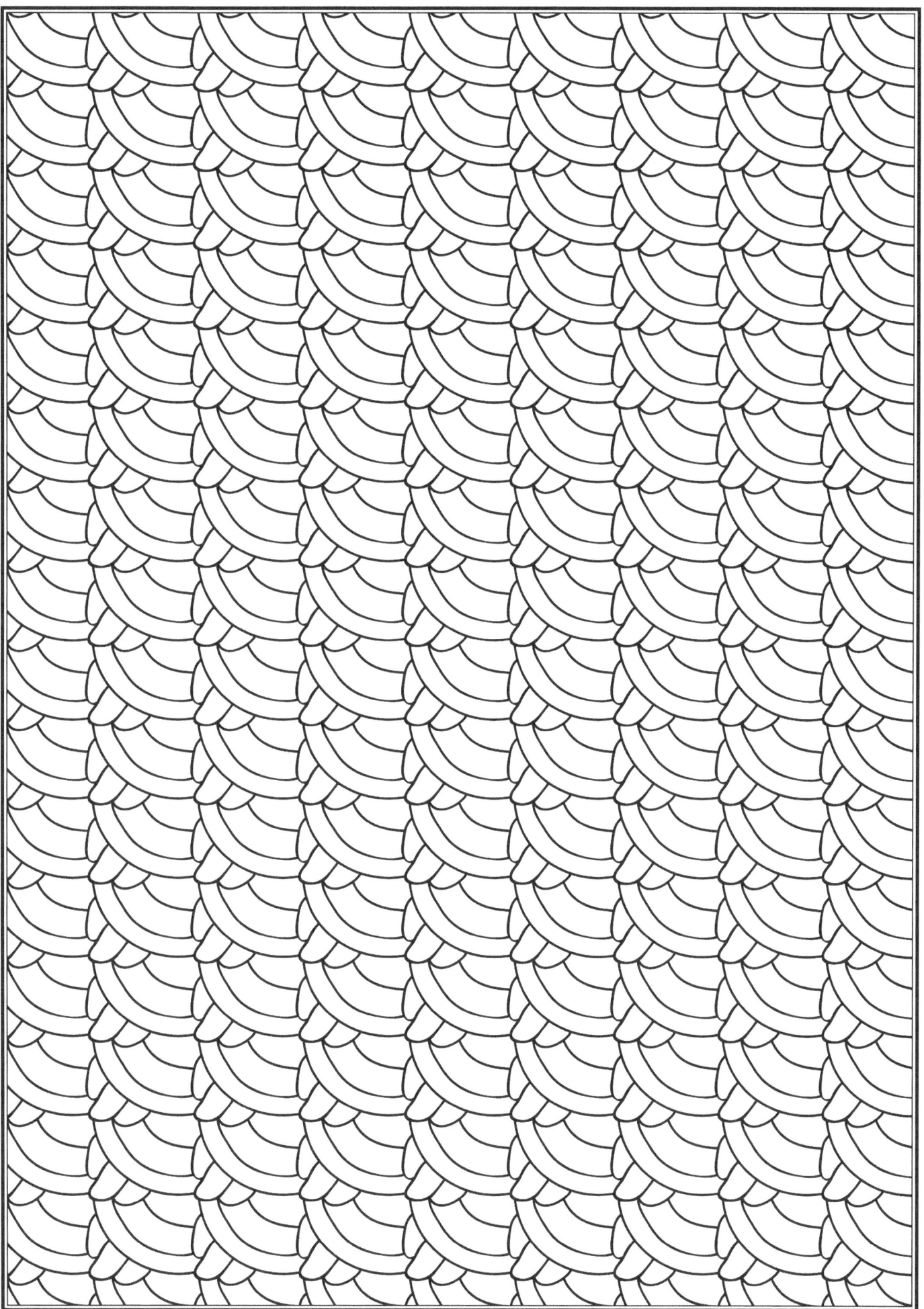

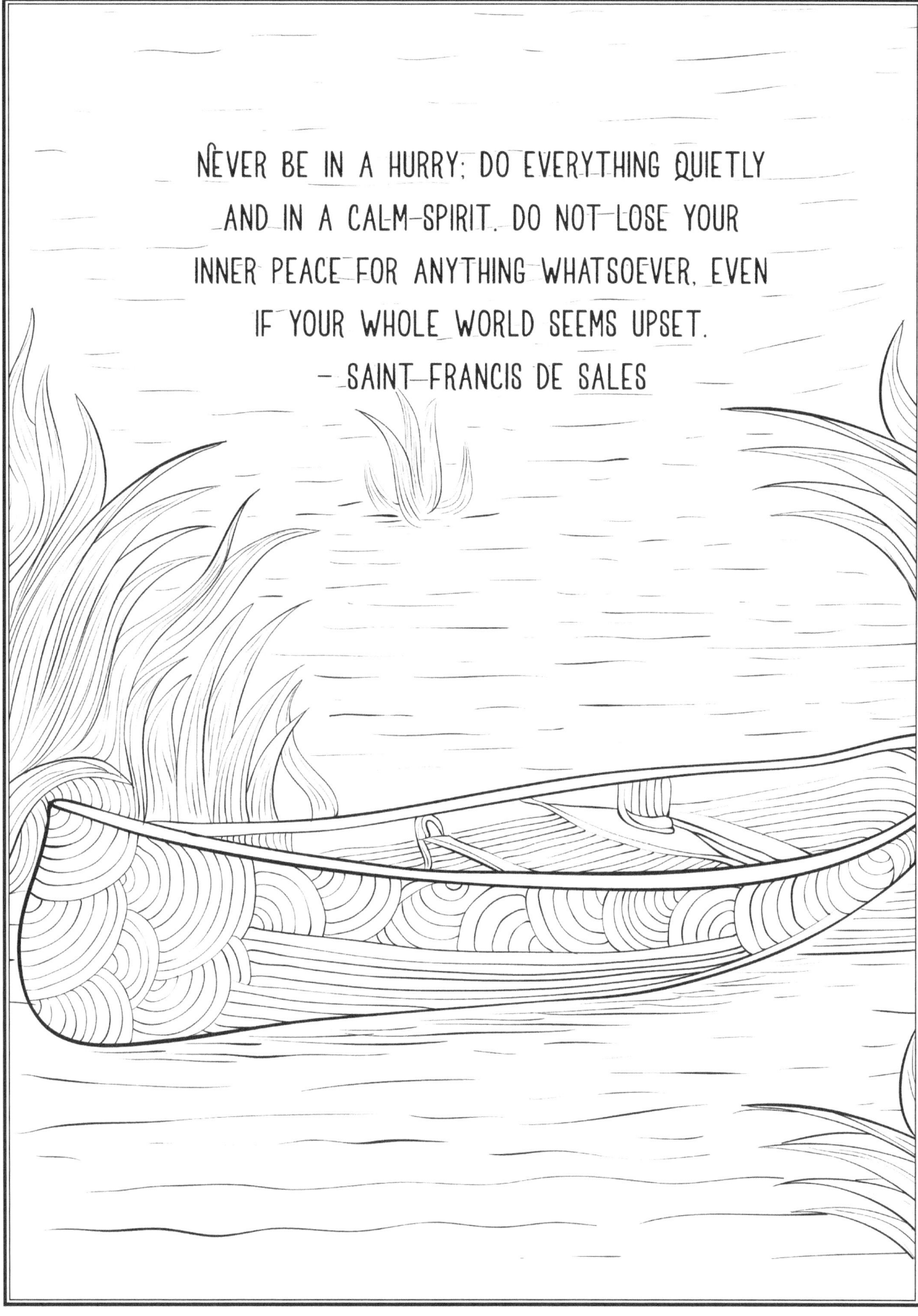

NEVER BE IN A HURRY; DO EVERYTHING QUIETLY
AND IN A CALM-SPIRIT. DO NOT LOSE YOUR
INNER PEACE FOR ANYTHING WHATSOEVER, EVEN
IF YOUR WHOLE WORLD SEEMS UPSET.
– SAINT FRANCIS DE SALES

Many a calm river begins as a turbulent waterfall, yet none hurtles and foams all the way to the sea.

-Mikhail Lermontov

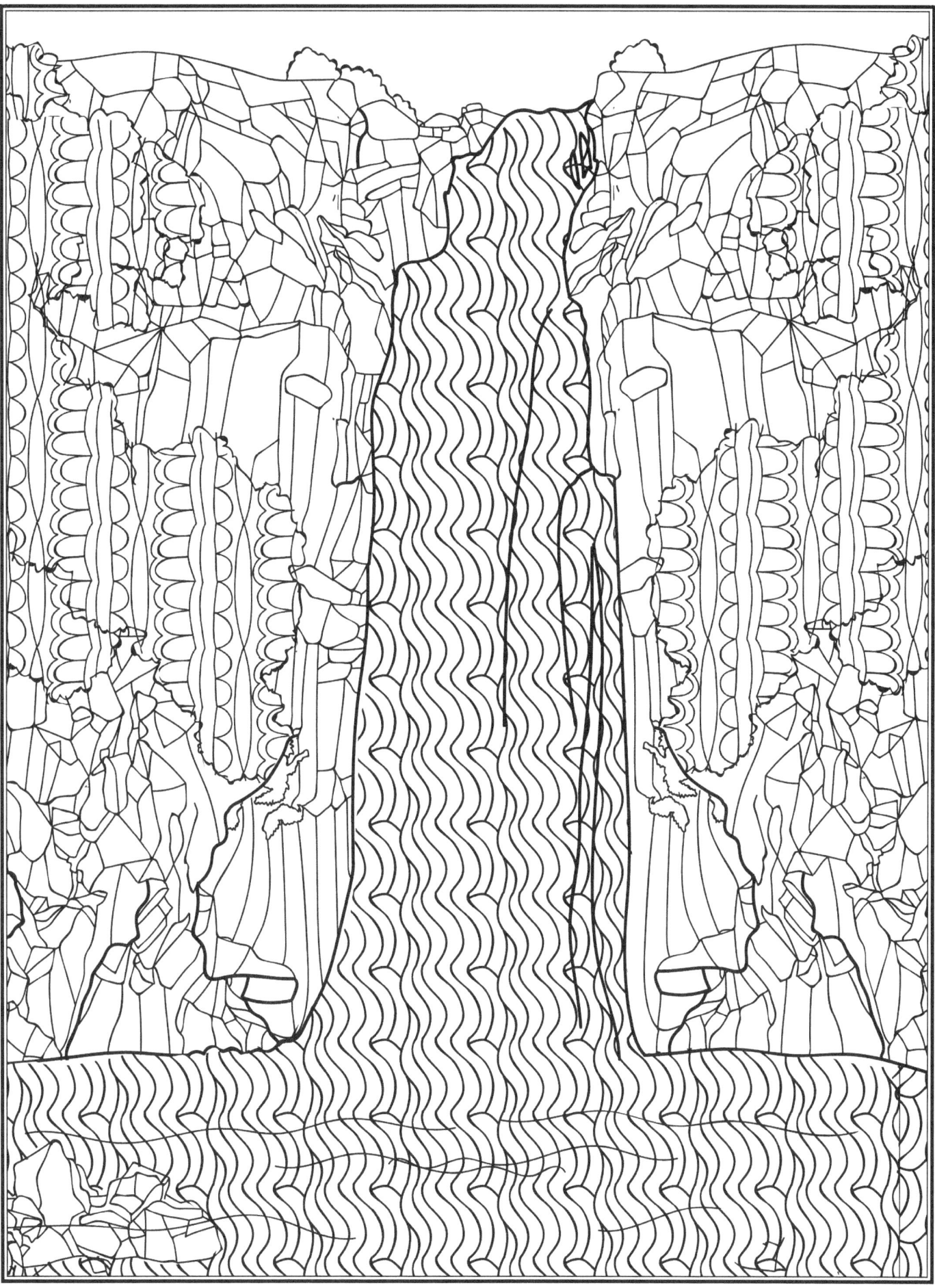

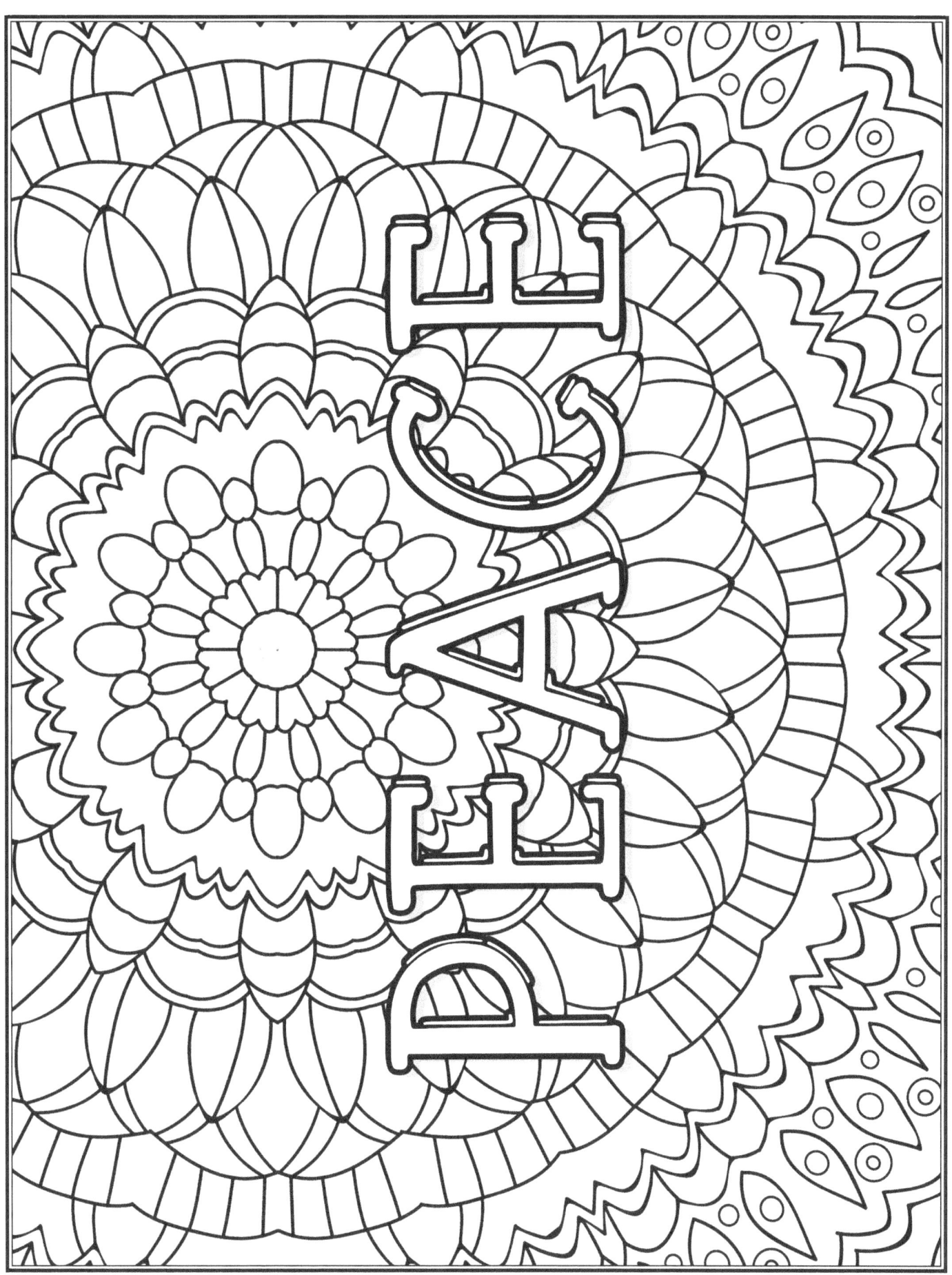

To have faith is to trust yourself to the water. When you swim you don't grab hold of the water, because if you do you will sink and drown. Instead you relax, and float.
- Alan Watts

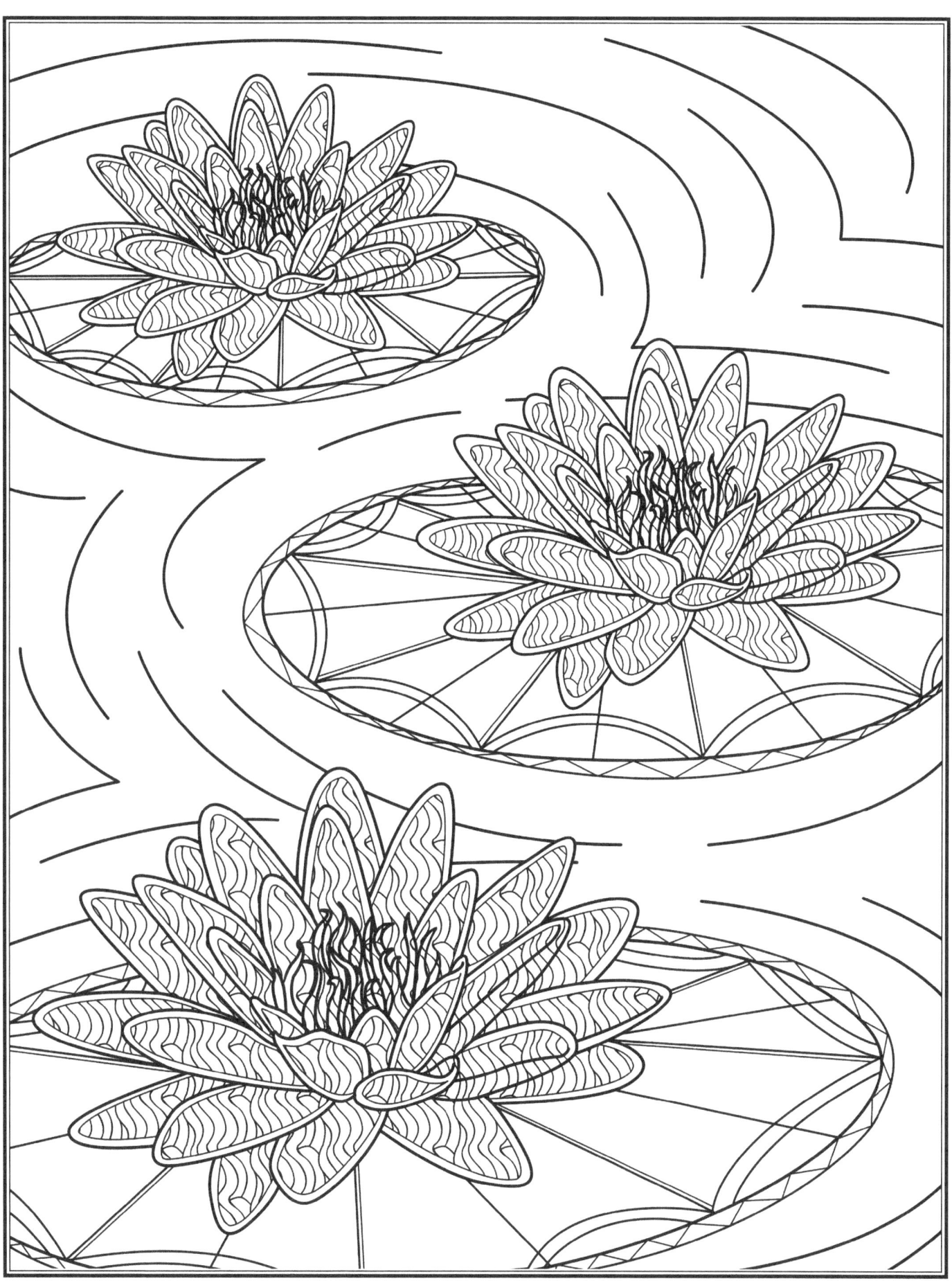

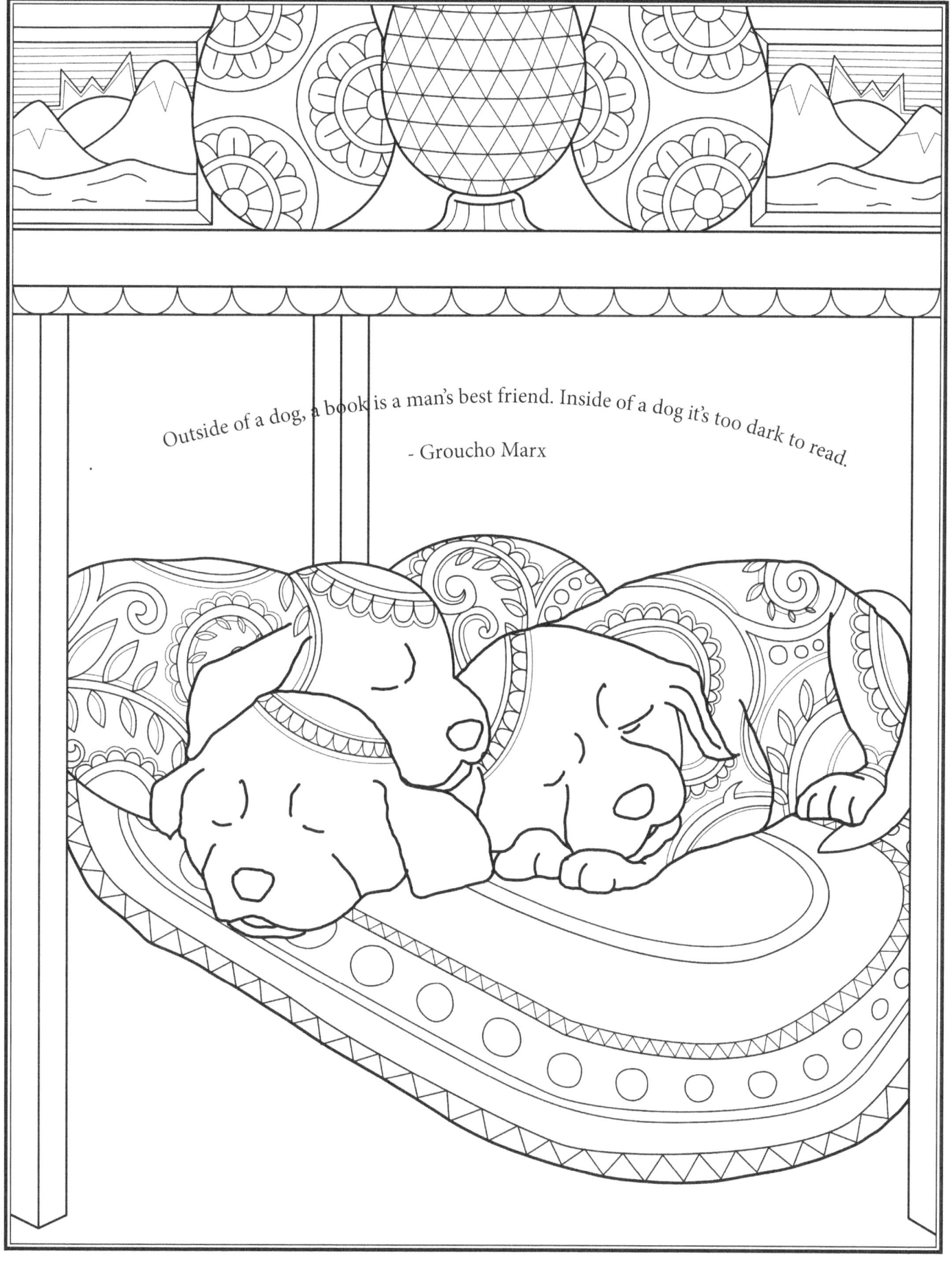

Outside of a dog, a book is a man's best friend. Inside of a dog it's too dark to read.

- Groucho Marx

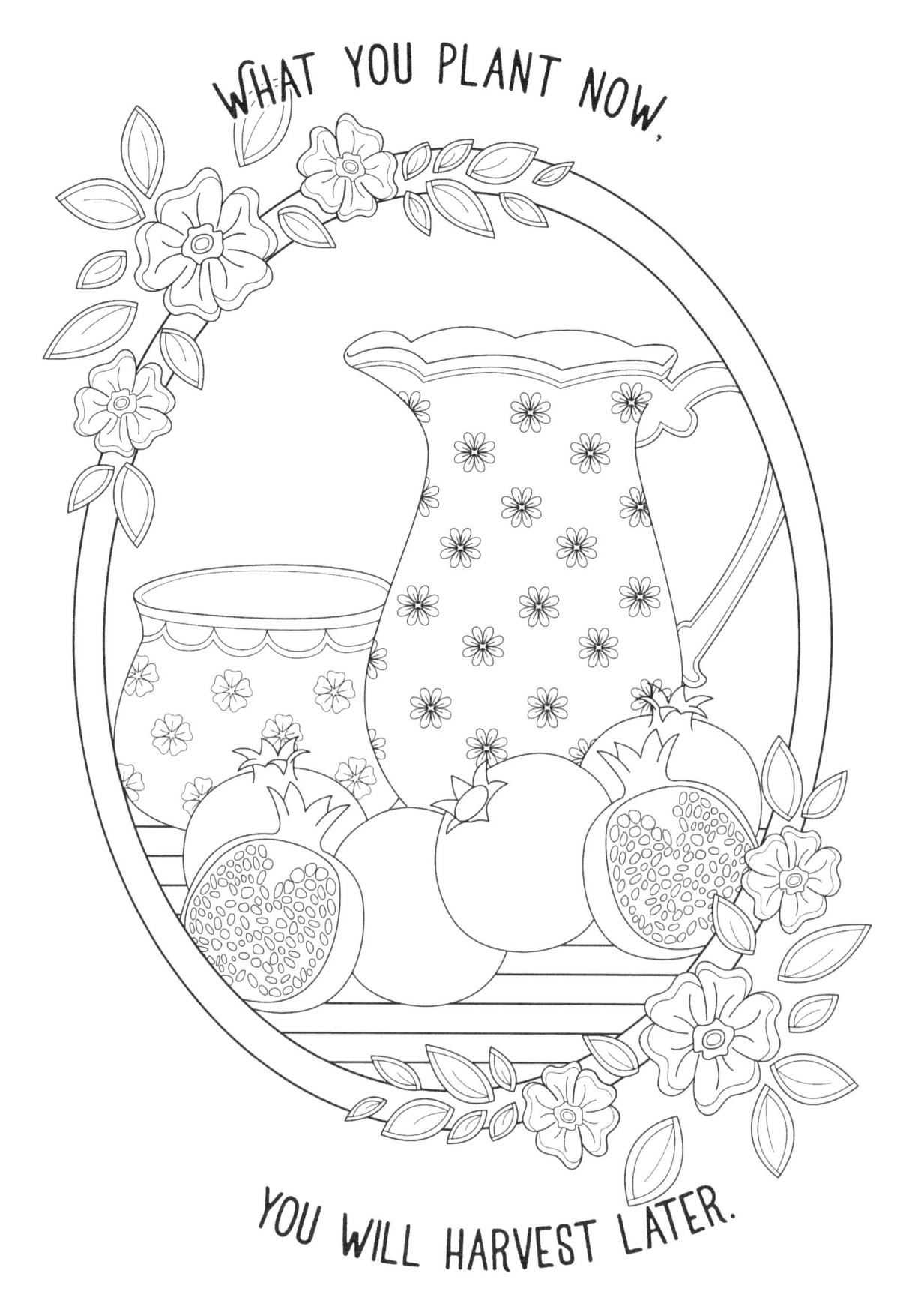

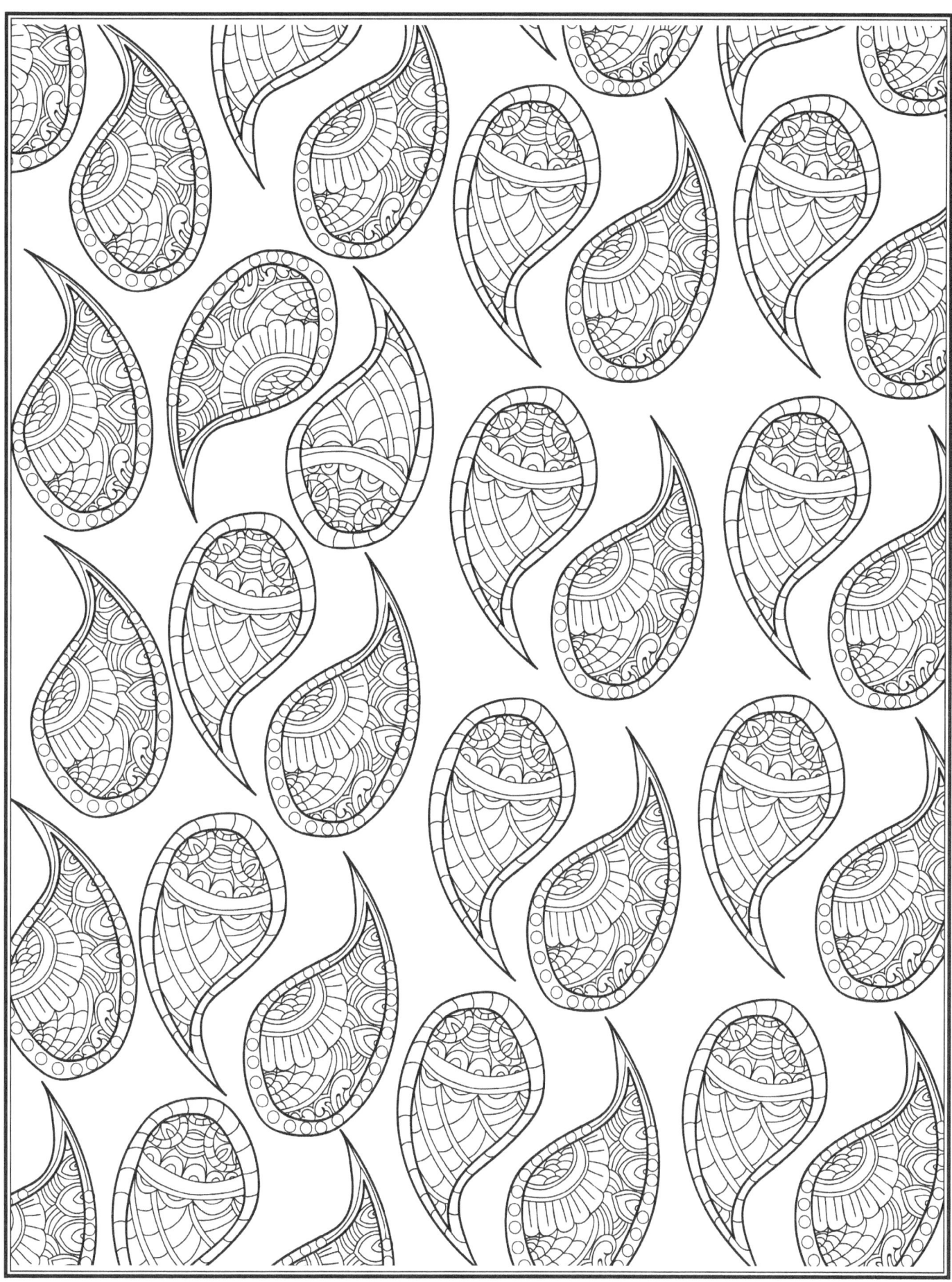

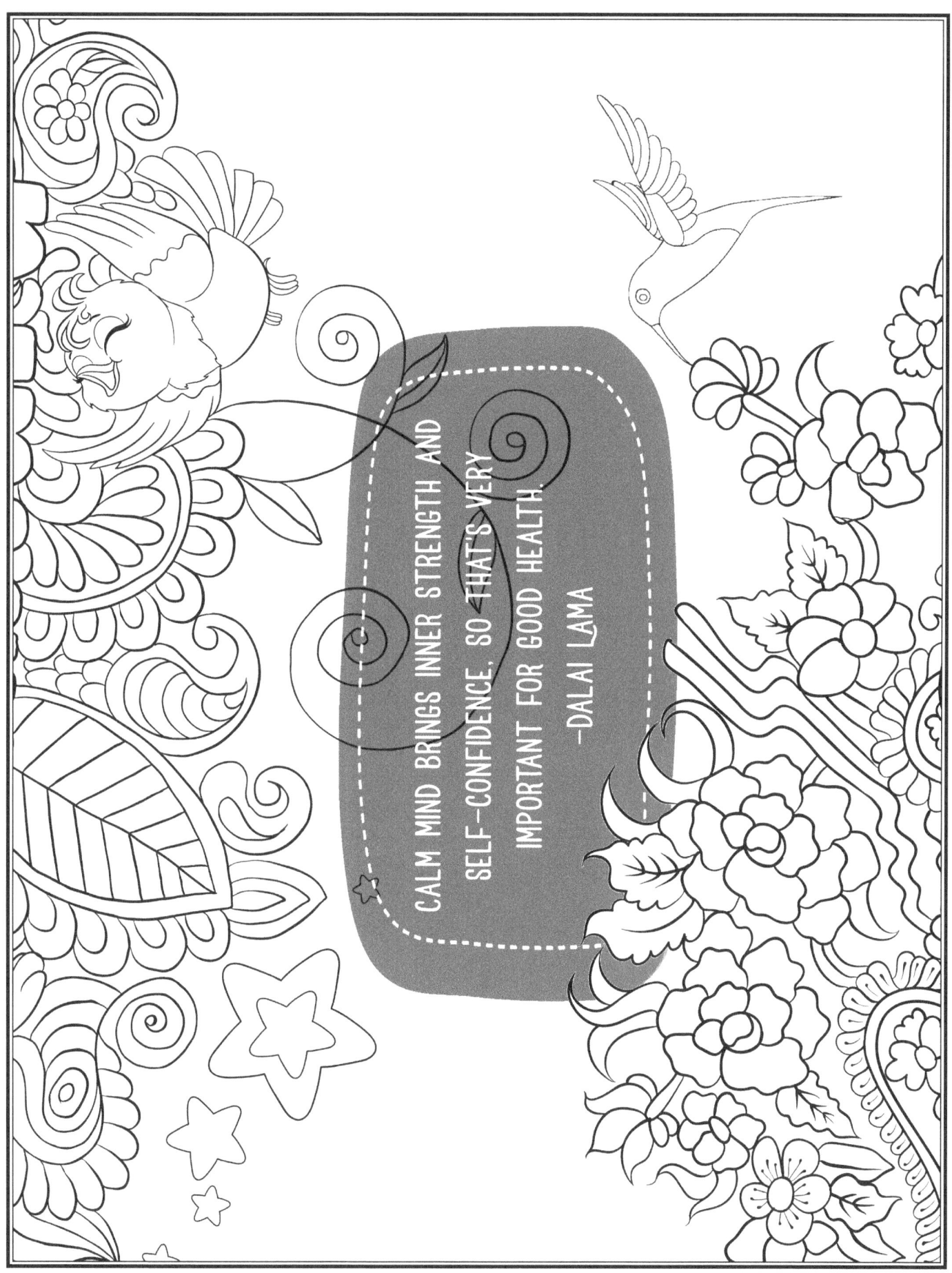

CALM MIND BRINGS INNER STRENGTH AND SELF-CONFIDENCE, SO THAT'S VERY IMPORTANT FOR GOOD HEALTH.

-DALAI LAMA

www.ingramcontent.com/pod-product-compliance
Lightning Source LLC
Chambersburg PA
CBHW080640190526
45169CB00009B/3444